The Alpha Course Leaders' Training Manual

for leaders and helpers on the Alpha course

First published 1993   Revised edition August 1998
Reprinted August 1999 Reprinted twice 2000
Revised May 2001   Reprinted February 2002
Reprinted June 2002   Reprinted October 2002
Reprinted March 2003   Reprinted August 2003
Revised December 2003

This edition for Senior Alpha first published 2005

© Alpha International
Published by Alpha International
Holy Trinity Brompton, Brompton Road, London SW7 1JA
Printed in the UK by TPS Print Ltd
5 Tunnel Avenue, Greenwich, London SE10 0SL
Telephone: 020 8269 1222

Contents

1. Leading Small Groups

Introduction

The overall purpose of the small group, along with the course as a whole, is to help to bring people into a relationship with Jesus Christ.

Jesus himself said that where two or three are gathered in his name he is there also (Matthew 18:20).

- A group of about 12 is the ideal size.
- Jesus chose a group of 12 (Matthew 4:18–22).
- Each small group is made up of two leaders, two helpers and approximately eight guests.

The six subsidiary aims of the small group:

1. TO DISCUSS

To discuss the talk and issues arising out of the talk. It is vital to give people the opportunity to respond to what they have heard and the opportunity to ask questions.

With some groups you may never get beyond discussion to Bible study. This applies especially to groups of non-churchgoers or non-Christians.

a) Practical details

- Arrange chairs so that everyone is comfortable
- Leader can see everyone
- Light is good
- Check ventilation
- Keeping time – aim to start and finish on time

b) Some groups are ruined by one of two things:

- Weak leadership – not properly prepared, lets one

person do all the talking

- Too dominant leadership - does all the talking, instead of giving people the freedom to speak and to say what is on their minds

c) Ask simple questions

- If you feel that the group is not ready for Bible study but discussion is not flowing very easily, possible questions to start discussion are attached in Appendix I

- Two basic questions:
  - What do you think?
  - What do you feel?

- Avoid being patronising. Guests may be new to Christianity, but they are not new to life. Treat everyone with respect and interest

- Direct questions back to the group 'What does everyone else think?'

d) Be prepared for discussion group questions

- Resource: **Searching Issues** by Nicky Gumbel, the seven issues most often raised on Alpha.

2. TO MODEL BIBLE STUDY

To study the Bible as a group, aiming to understand the passage and its context, to apply it to our own situation, and to hear God speak through it. Don't do it until everyone is ready. Don't give a talk - encourage others to talk. Aim to motivate the group to start to read the Bible alone.

a) When you start

- Even if Bible study is planned, give everyone an opportunity to ask questions arising out of the talk or other questions on their minds.

b) If the group is ready for Bible study, the leader needs to prepare the passage carefully

(For suggested passages see Appendix I - but be free to study any passage which you think is appropriate)

- Read passage (different versions): make sure you understand it
- Spot difficult verses: make sure you know answers from commentary

c) Read passage

- Explain where it comes in the Bible
- Read either verse by verse or whole passage read by one good reader. Be sensitive to those who might not want to read

d) Give a short introduction

- Give in a sentence the main theme of the passage
- Explain at once any obviously difficult or ambiguous words (very little to be gained by asking 'What does dissimulation mean?')
- Avoid (at all times) spiritual clichés, long words and Christian jargon which exclude the non-Christian and the new Christian

e) Get people talking

- Work out your questions carefully - short and simple (some examples are set out in Appendix I)

  - Not too hard

  - Not too easy – 'Who died for us?'

  - Not too vague – 'What is the difference between verses 7 and 17?'

- Ask open ended questions, eg 'What?', 'How?', 'Who?' and 'Why?' Not closed questions (Yes/No answers)

- Aim to bring everyone into the discussion. Welcome any contribution from a quieter member

- Basic questions:

  - 'What does it say?'

  - 'What does it mean?'

  - 'How does it apply?'

- Learn as well as teach. Do not impose your own ideas

- Try not to answer your own questions yourself!

- Do not repeat someone's comment unless it needs alteration. If you cannot answer the question do not bluff. Admit ignorance and either tackle the question afterwards or make a note and bring the answer next time. Better still, get someone else to do it!

f) Encouraging the group

- Smile(!) and look interested
- Respond verbally to guests' comments:
    - 'How interesting'
    - 'I have never heard that before!'
    - 'It might mean that...'

3. TO LEARN TO PRAY TOGETHER

a) Opening prayer

- Either by you, or better still, by a member of the group
- To avoid embarrassment:

       –   Put words into their mouth: 'Will you ask God to give us wisdom to understand this passage . . ?'

or –   Ask someone beforehand to lead in prayer, and then say to the group, 'I have asked X to open in prayer'

b)   End with prayer (if appropriate)

       –   Long eloquent prayers may be impressive but they discourage others from praying

       –   Ideal prayer! 'Father . . . (short sentence) . . . for Jesus' sake, Amen'

4. TO DEVELOP LASTING FRIENDSHIPS WITHIN THE BODY OF CHRIST

- The main reason why people stay in the church
- Get to know each person well
- Icebreaker games eg name game (first night)
- Act as hosts

- Facilitate conversations
- Meet together during the week

5.   TO LEARN TO MINISTER TO ONE ANOTHER

- Gifts of the Spirit

6.   TO TRAIN OTHERS TO LEAD

- Delegation without training leads to disappointment (2 Timothy 2:2)

2. Pastoral Care

Introduction

a) Jesus' words to Peter

- Mark 1:17
- John 21:22

b) Example of Jesus himself

- Luke 13:34

c) Pastoral care involves heart and hands

- Psalm 78:72

'We proclaim him, admonishing and teaching everyone with all wisdom, so that we may present everyone perfect in Christ. To this end I labour, struggling with all his energy, which so powerfully works in me.' (Colossians 1:28–29)

1.   AIM

'. . . so that we may present everyone perfect [ie mature] in Christ'
(Colossians 1:28)

a)   Everyone

- Every single person on Alpha to be looked after
- Leader to divide up group to take pastoral responsibility for members
- The system must ensure every person is cared for
- Pray daily for each person

b)   Spiritual maturity

- Not just Alpha
- Follow up: home group
- Role in church
- Use of gifts

c)   Maturity in Christ

- We do not want to attach people to ourselves
  - but to Christ

- Good parents encourage independence

2.   METHOD

'We proclaim him, admonishing and teaching everyone with all wisdom . . .' (Colossians 1:28)

We grow in maturity as intimacy with the Lord and our knowledge of him grows

a)   Lead people to Jesus

- Resource: Why Jesus?

b)   Encourage them to grow in their relationship with Jesus

- Bible study/prayer

- Christian books
  (see end of each chapter in The Alpha Course Manual)

- Tapes

c) Encourage them to grow in their relationships within the body of Christ

- Alpha evenings
- Sundays
- Telephone
- Giving lifts to one another

General Attitude

a) Be an encourager

- (1 Thessalonians 5:11)
- Expressing warmth and responsiveness

b) Be a listener (not always a teacher)

- (James 1:19–26)
- Listening gives people their dignity

c) Be a peacemaker

- (Matthew 5:9)

- Reconciling differences, relieving tension and exploring reasons for differences (diplomatically)

3. COMMITMENT

'To this end I labour, struggling with all his energy, which so powerfully works in me' (Colossians 1:29)

Our responsibility and God's grace

a) Our responsibility
- 'Struggling'
    - commitment to pray
    - hard work
    - effort
    - overcoming tiredness
    - not talking to old friends but welcoming new people
    - efficiency with jobs

–   overcoming disappointment

b) God's grace

'. . . with all his energy . . .' (Colossians 1:29)

'full of faith and of the Holy Spirit' (Acts 6:5)

- You need to receive
  –   Try to allow the Spirit of God to speak to you during the talks and fill you during worship/ministry

but • Then be ready to serve

- Use every gift:
  –   Evangelism
  –   Teaching
  –   Pastoring
  –   Prophetic - hearing God

3. Ministry on Alpha

Introduction

'Ministry' is used in several different senses in the New Testament

Includes everything done on Alpha

'Meeting the needs of others on the basis of God's resources.'
(John Wimber's definition of ministry)

Co-operation between God and us (Exodus 14:16, 21–22)

Many opportunities for ministry during the course

eg weekend (Saturday evening and Sunday morning)
Healing evening

The five values for ministry

1. THE MINISTRY OF THE HOLY SPIRIT

a)   When we ask the Holy Spirit to come, he comes

   - Get our perspective right (Luke 10:17–20)

   - The branch must look principally at the vine and not at the fruit

b)   Because it is his ministry we aim for simplicity and truthfulness in all aspects of our prayers for people. Avoid all intensity

c)   Stay facing the person you are praying for and ask the Holy Spirit to come. Welcome him when you see signs of his working and wait on God as you pray for further directions!

d)   Silently ask God what he wants to do . . . to say . . . how to encourage and impart gifts

e)   Ask what is happening

   - 'Do you sense God saying something?'

   - 'What do you feel is happening?'

2. BIBLICAL AUTHORITY

a) The Spirit of God and the written word of God never conflict

- The truth sets us free (John 8:32)

b) Build on biblical truths and promises, eg

- Repentance (Psalm 51)
- Fear (Psalm 91)
- Anxiety (Philippians 4:6–7)
- Guidance (Psalm 37:5)
- Temptation (1 Corinthians 10:13)

c) Say how you are going to pray and encourage faith in a particular promise of God

(Hold on to God's promises. One aspect of faith is the finding of a promise of God and daring to believe it!)

3. THE DIGNITY OF THE INDIVIDUAL

a) Confidentiality is essential

b)   Pray for people in relaxed surroundings
     (either on your own or in pairs)

c)   Affirm – do not condemn

d)   Faith – do not place additional burdens on them

e)   Allow them freedom to come back!

f)   Take time to sort out difficulties of understanding, belief,
     and assurance

g)   Lead to Christ (resource: Why Jesus?)

h)   Fullness of the Spirit eg

   - 'Am I quite ready?'

   - 'I am unworthy'

   - I could never speak in another language'

   - 1 Corinthians 14:2,4,14 & Matthew 7:11

i)   Encourage the person to start to speak in another language
     –   tell him/her you will do so yourself

4. HARMONIOUS Relationships

'May they be brought to complete unity to let the world know that you sent me and have loved them even as you have loved me'
(John 17:23)

a)   Lack of unity, love and forgiveness hinders the work of the Spirit

b)   One person should take a lead and be seen to do so with the prayerful help of others

5. THE BODY OF CHRIST

a)   The Christian community is the place where long-term healing and spiritual growth take place under the protective umbrella of the authority of a church

b)   Keep in touch

- Warn against possible increased temptation

- Refuse to consider that 'nothing has happened'

Ephesians 5:18 – go on being filled with the Spirit

Appendix I

SUGGESTED SMALL GROUP STRUCTURE

Here are a few suggestions for each small group time. The practical points should be useful each week. Obviously, the discussion questions will not be necessary if the conversation arises naturally. You would probably only use one per topic, and hope to let things flow from there. They are intended to be as open and un-threatening as possible. They are only suggestions, and do use any method or questions that you find helpful. You can also use the optional Bible studies in more advanced groups.

HELPFUL GENERAL QUESTIONS:

How did you respond to the talk?

What did you feel about the talk?

What did you think about the talk?

Did anything that was said particularly speak to you or surprise you?

What issues were raised for you by the talk?

Is this a new subject for anyone?

Note: The Introductory Session 'Christianity: Boring, Untrue & Irrelevant?' is given at the celebration supper at the end of the course. Talks 8, 9, 10 and 15 are given on the weekend away.

Week 1 – Who is Jesus?

PRACTICAL

1) Welcome everyone to the group.

2) Send an address form around the group for the guests to fill in. Explain that this is a great help administratively but not necessary if a guest is uncomfortable.

3) Icebreakers (if appropriate).

   a) Name Game

   Explain that this is a silly game – but the best way for everyone to learn each others' names the first night.

   To play the name game:

   i) Each person tries to think of an adjective that would describe them. It must also have the same first letter as their name. For example 'Jovial John' or 'Happy Helen'.

ii)   Each person says what their name is and why. For example: Jovial John is jovial because he has a hearty laugh.

iii)   Each person has a go at repeating all the names of the group from memory.

b)   Either

If you were stranded on a desert island what three things would you take with you?

or   If your house was on fire and you could go back and get one thing what would you get?

or   What is your earliest memory?

c)   What made you decide to do an Alpha course? Start with someone who is likely to admit they are an atheist/agnostic. This gives the rest of the group permission to say what they really think. (If you start with someone who turns out to be an enthusiastic Christian already, it may be harder for the rest of the group to be honest about their lack of belief.)

DISCUSSION

1)   Before you heard the talk, what was your concept of Jesus? Has it changed? If so, in what way?

2)   What do people think about Jesus?

3)   If you had a chance to meet him how would you feel and what would you say to him?

Week 2 – Why Did Jesus Die?

PRACTICAL

Introduce any new guests. Pass around the address list. Add new names and addresses and correct any mistakes from the previous week.

DISCUSSION

This is often the week when the subject of 'suffering' arises (see **Searching Issues**, Chapter 1).

1) What is your reaction to the crucifixion?

2) Do you feel that sin is an outdated concept or is it something you can relate to?

3) How do you respond to the word 'sin' and the word 'forgiveness'?

4)   Would you agree that sin is addictive? What do you see as the consequences of sin, if any?

OPTIONAL BIBLE STUDY

Luke 15:11–24 The parable of the prodigal son

a)   Why do you think that the son decided to leave home? What was he hoping for?

- 'Wild living' (v.13)

- 'Give me' (v.11) selfishness/sin

b)   What was life like in the far country?

- Wasting his life (v.13)

- Began to see the need (v.14)

- Severe famine (v.14)

- Hunger (v.15)

- Loneliness (v.15)

c)   How does this compare with your experience of life?

d) What made him decide to go home?

- Thinks about situation
- 'He came to his senses' (v.17)

e) What does he decide to do?

- Act of the will (v.18)
- Action (v.20)

f) What does the picture of the Father tell us about what God is like? (vv. 20–24)

Week 3 – How Can I Be Sure of My Faith?

PRACTICAL

Introduce any new guests. Pass around the address list. Add new names and addresses and correct any mistakes from the previous week.

This is a good week to mention the Alpha Weekend/Day for the first time. Tell the group the dates.

DISCUSSION

You may well find that people have a question, for example, about other religions (see **Searching Issues**, Chapter 2).

1) What would you write on a form where it asked your religion?

2) Do you associate love or fear with God?

3) When it is said that Christianity will make a change in your character, how do you feel?

4) What does the idea of a relationship with God suggest to you?

OPTIONAL BIBLE STUDY

1 Peter 1:3–8

a) What do you think Peter means by 'new birth'? (v.3)

b) What does the future hold for Christians? (v.4) (compare hopes of the world)

c) How can we be so sure about the future?

- Resurrection
- Shielded by God's power (v.5)

d) In what light should we see our problems?

- Relative shortness (v.6)

- Their purpose (v.7)

e) What do we learn from verse 8 about our relationship with Jesus Christ?

- Our love for him

- The joy

Week 4 – Why and How Should I Read the Bible?

PRACTICAL

This is a good week to encourage people about the Alpha Weekend/Day. Mention the cost and the possibility of bursaries.

DISCUSSION

1)   Have you ever/recently read the Bible? How did you get on?

2)   Have you ever read a modern translation?

3)   Have you read anything in the Bible which has corrected an aspect of your beliefs or behaviour?

4)   What do you feel about the suggestion that the Bible is the 'manual for life'?

5) In the talk, the Bible was also described as a 'love letter'. Have you experienced that, and in what way?

6) 'What the Scriptures said, God said.' Do you share that view?

OPTIONAL BIBLE STUDY

Mark 4:1–8, 13–20 The parable of the sower

'Parable': Putting one thing alongside another by way of comparison or illustration

Key = Jesus is not speaking about different people but about all of us at different times in our lives

a) The hard-hearted (vv.4, 15)

- What was the problem?

- What is the difference between hearing the word and responding?

- Can you think of occasions when you have heard the Bible, read or heard talks/sermons and they have made no impact at all or only a very superficial impact on your life?

b)   The faint-hearted (vv.5–6; 16–17)

- What was the problem?

- What sort of things do you think Jesus meant by 'trouble' and 'persecution' (opposition)?

- What do you think the roots are?

  – Roots cannot be seen - the things we do in secret such as Bible reading, prayer, giving etc.

c)   The half-hearted (vv.7, 18)

- What was the problem?

- How long did it take for the problem to become apparent?

- How do we avoid allowing the worries of this life, the deceitfulness of wealth and the desire for other things choking the word?

d)   The whole-hearted (vv.8, 20)

- What does God promise to those who persevere?

- What do you think the crop is?

Week 5 – Why and How Do I Pray?

PRACTICAL

Remind the group about the Alpha Weekend/Day. Ask someone who has benefited from a previous weekend to describe their experience. Take further names and collect payment.

DISCUSSION

1)   Have you ever tried praying? What happened?

2)   How do you find the idea of God answering prayer?

3)   Have you ever seen coincidences happen when you pray?

4)   In the talk, various reasons for praying are given. Which of these do you relate to and why?

OPTIONAL BIBLE STUDY
Matthew 6: 5–13 The Lord's Prayer

a) Are verses 5–6 suggesting that it's wrong to pray in public? What is Jesus really getting at?

- Need for sincerity

b) What can you do to reduce the distractions that get in the way of your time alone with God? (v.6)

- Need for secrecy

c) What are the differences between pagan and Christian prayer? (v.7)

d) What is the difference between the repetition in prayer which Jesus denounces and the persistence in prayer which he recommends? (v.7)

- Need for simplicity

e) How could you apply the requests of the Lord's Prayer more to your own life?

- Need for structure

f) Take time to talk about any answers to prayer that you have seen recently.

Week 6 – How Does God Guide Us?

PRACTICAL

Arrange lifts for the Alpha Weekend/Day if necessary.

DISCUSSION

1) Does anyone think they might have experienced God's guidance in the last few weeks?

2) How do you respond to the idea of God having a plan for you?

3) What are the ways that God speaks to people today? Have you experienced this?

4) What should we do if we believe we have made a mess of our lives?

OPTIONAL BIBLE STUDY

Proverbs 16:1–9

a)   What conditions does God attach to guiding us? (vv.3, 5, 7)

- Confide in God
- No room for pride or independence
- Obedience

b)   What promises of success does he offer? (vv.6b–8)

- Avoidance of evil
- Peaceful life
- Note: not necessarily material success

c)   How does this picture compare with your own experience?

d)   With so much confusion in the world how do we know that God can do it? (vv.1, 4, 9)

- God is sovereign
- He is in control

Alpha Weekend – Saturday am

BIBLE STUDY

1 Corinthians 12:1–11

a) Has anyone heard of or had any experience of spiritual gifts?

b) What spiritual gifts are there? (vv.8–10) Where do these gifts come from? (v.11)

- List gifts and explain them

- All from God

c) How do you feel about the idea of God giving us supernatural gifts?

d) Does everybody have the same gifts? (vv. 4–6)

- Different gifts, works, and service but same God

e)   Why does God give spiritual gifts to people?   (v.7)

- For the common good

- Not for our glory

f)   Mention that there may be an opportunity in the afternoon to hear more on this subject.

Alpha Weekend – Sunday am

Ask each member of the group to describe their experience of the weekend so far. Rejoice and reassure as necessary.

Week 7 – How Can I Resist Evil?

PRACTICAL

Start the small group time by asking of people's experiences of the Alpha Weekend/Day. This gives the guests the opportunity to verbalise what God has done in their lives. It can be a great encouragement to the group. Remember to include those who did not go on the Weekend/Day in the discussion.

DISCUSSION

1)   Do you believe in the supernatural/black magic/the occult?

2)   Before today, did you have a concept of the devil?
      Has it changed?

3)   Why do you think bad things happen?

4)   Why do you think the world is in such a mess?

OPTIONAL BIBLE STUDY

Ephesians 6:10–20 The armour of God

a) What do verses 11 and 12 tell us about the nature of the struggle in which we are involved?

- subtlety of attack: 'devil's schemes' (v.11)

- power (v.12)

- brutality (v.12)

b) What do you think Paul means by 'the day of evil'? (v.13) (Discuss times of strong attack)

c) What do you think the pieces of armour represent? How do we acquire them?

Truth: Bible, books, tapes etc

Righteousness: Doing what is right/clear conscience

The gospel of peace: Telling others

Faith: Opposite of cynicism/scepticism/doubt etc.

Helmet of salvation: Knowing in your head that you are saved/assurance

Word of God: Regular Bible reading

Prayer: Regular prayer and especially for opportunities to tell others (vv 19–20) eg Celebration Lunch/Supper!

Week 8 – Why and How Should We Tell Others?

PRACTICAL

If the dates and details of the Celebration Lunch/Supper do not come up naturally in the discussion this is a good time to mention them. Invitation cards can be handed out too. If possible, aim to pray together as a group at the end of this week.

DISCUSSION

1) If you did not know anything about Christianity, how would you like to be told about it?

2) Have you told any of your friends/family/colleagues at work about doing the Alpha course? What was their reaction?

3) What do you think/feel about the idea of telling others?

OPTIONAL BIBLE STUDY

John 4:1–26 Jesus talks with a Samaritan woman

a)   What do we know about the woman?

b)   How did Jesus initiate the conversation/contact? (v.7)

c)   How did Jesus present the gospel? Why did he present it like this to her? (vv.10, 13–14)

d)   What does he mean by 'living water'/ 'springs of water welling up to eternal life'?

e)   Why does she start talking about 'mountains'? (v.20)

f)   What does Jesus do about the red herring?

g)   What does it mean to be 'presented with Jesus?' (v.26)

Week 9 – Does God Heal Today?

PRACTICAL

Remind people about the Celebration Lunch/Supper. Try to work out approximately how many people will be coming including small group members and guests.

DISCUSSION AND PRAYER

Ask if anyone in the group thinks that a 'word of knowledge' may have been appropriate for them. At the same time ask if anyone would like prayer for any other issue. This is a good time to clear up any general issues about healing. If there are lots of people, split into men and women at this stage.

Pray for people according to the ministry guidelines in this manual. Be prepared for someone who may want to give their life to Christ. Affirm those who do want to be prayed for and those who do not.

Week 10 – What About the Church?

PRACTICAL

Remind the group about the Celebration Lunch/Supper. Try to finalise numbers.

Make a date for a small group reunion.

DISCUSSION AND PRAYER

1)   Go round the group asking each person to summarise what they have learnt and experienced over the duration of the course.
(Try to start and end with an enthusiastic person!)

2)   Ask the group what they would like to do next. Try to encourage them to stay as a group.

3)   Ask each of them if there is anything they would like prayer for.

4)   Pray - it's a good idea to finish the final evening with prayer.

QUESTIONS FOR FURTHER DISCUSSION

1)   If someone says the word **church or Christian**, what comes to mind?

2)   Look back over the course. Has your view changed?

3)   Now, shall we look forward? In what way (if any) do you plan to continue what you've started on this Alpha course?

Appendix II

Preparation Meeting

INTRODUCTION

1) Every job is vitally important. If you are unable to carry out the job you have been allocated, please let the administrator know.

2) It is important to remember that we are the hosts and should make newcomers feel welcome.

3) It would be appreciated if everyone stayed to help clear up at the end of each evening.

4) Please ensure that everyone attends the admin/prayer meeting before the start of the course as there are often important notices to give out.

NORMAL SCHEDULE

12.15 pm   Admin/prayer meeting for all helpers and leaders. Everyone should know exactly where their group is meeting a) for lunch and b) for small groups. For the first two weeks, the admin/prayer meeting for helpers will start at 12 noon.

12.30 pm   Admin/prayer meeting ends. All leaders and helpers to go and welcome people.

1.00 pm   The administrators should meet people as they arrive and should allocate them to a group, introducing them to a runner/welcomer who will quickly take them to the label desk and then to their group.

BOOKSTALL OPEN DURING LUNCH

1.00 pm   One group leader to stay at lunch meeting point. Other helpers can act as runners/welcomers collecting people as they arrive, getting them a label and introducing them to remaining group leader.

51

(In practice many people may have friends they want to talk to/sit with, but they should be encouraged to remain with their group.)

Lunch should be served as quickly as possible to avoid queues and to allow time for people to chat over lunch.

1.30 pm   Encourage groups to move seats into semi-circle for notices, worship and talk.

2.45 pm   Talk ends.

BOOKSTALL SHOULD BE OPEN

Coffee

2.55 pm   Helpers should encourage people to join small groups promptly and show them to where to go. NB do not forget those who were not there previous week.

3.05 pm   Small Groups begin.

3.45 pm   Small Groups end.

The Alpha Course

Registration Form

Please use this form to register your Alpha course if it is not already listed in Alpha News. Or register online by visiting: alpha.org.

Registering your course is free of charge and enables us to list it in Alpha News and on our website.

COURSE CONTACT

Title   First Name

Surname

Address

Post/Zip Code   Country

Telephone

Email

CHURCH LEADER

Title   First Name
_____   _____

Surname
_____

Address
_____

_____

Post/Zip Code   Country
_____   _____

Telephone
_____

Email
_____

CHURCH/ORGANISATION DETAILS

Church/Organisation Name
_____

Denomination
_____

Mailing Address
_____

_____

Country & Post/Zip Code
_____

Telephone
_____

Email
_____

Website

DATA PROTECTION POLICY

The information you provide on this form will only be used for purposes directly connected with the Alpha course. We never sell, rent or loan your personal information to others, although we sometimes pass your details to our Alpha Advisers and local conference organisers. We hold your details on computer under the terms of the Data Protection Act 1998.

☐ If you would prefer your details not to be given to our trusted Alpha Advisers and local conference organisers for Alpha related activities only, please tick this box.

☐ Please tick here if you don't want your name and daytime telephone number to be listed on our website search facility.

COURSE DETAILS

Course Name
_____

Course Denomination
_____

Course Town
_____
(as you would prefer it listed in Alpha News)

Course County/Province
_____

Course Post Code
_____

Country
_____

Date of first Alpha course at this church
_____

How many times has this church run Alpha?
_____

Type of Alpha course
_____

Average No of people attending your daytime course
_____

Average No of people attending your evening course
_____

Average No of people attending your Youth course:
_____

How do you give the course talks

☐ Video   ☐ Audio   ☐ Own Speakers   ☐ Combination